"Let's make a band."

"Let's make a band."

Dale makes a lute.

Dale makes a lute.

Dale makes tunes on his lute.

Dale makes tunes on his lute.

Kate gets a pipe.

Kate gets a pipe.

Kate can make a tune on a pipe.

Kate can make a tune on a pipe.

Max has a box.

Max has a box.

Max hits his box.

Max hits his box.

It makes a big "pop".

Pop, pop! Pop, pop!

It makes a big "pop".

Pop, pop! Pop, pop!

Reed will lead his band.

Reed will lead his band.

Dale makes tunes.

Dale makes tunes.

Kate makes tunes.

Kate makes tunes.

"Pop, pop," goes Max.

"Pop, pop," goes Max.

Muff hears a tune.

Muff wakes up and wags
his tail.

Muff hears a tune.

Muff wakes up and wags his tail.

Muff likes Reed's band.

Muff likes Reed's band.

It is a fine band.

It is a fine band.